SINGULARITY

John-Paris Kent lives in ⁚
three children. He hasn't h
ages but in 2011 his story *F*
by A.L. Kennedy at the Bridport Prize. In 2013 his poem
Ex-Girlfriends was also shortlisted by Roger McGough.

Singularity

John-Paris Kent

PRINTED BY SARSEN PRESS

A catalogue record for this book is available from the British Library.

© John-Paris Kent
First published Spring 2023

ISBN 978-1-7398332-8-2

Designed by Tim Underwood   timund@hotmail.com
Cover artwork by Chloe Kent
Printed by Sarsen Press   22 Hyde Street, Winchester, SO23 7DR

Contents

SINGULARITY

Half-painted Bathroom

What is was; and what it will be

Greek Statue

For a brief moment
I felt like a Greek statue
standing in the shower –

my teapot spout willy,
my right leg slightly bent,
my body set into itself
from all the heavy gardening
I'd just been doing

but then I did a wee,
a thick yellow wee

that trickled down the
inside of my leg

and in between the toes
on my right foot

and it was all ruined.

The 10:30 from Caerphilly to Pengam

There was so much truth
and beauty in that carriage

not a Grecian fucking urn

but fat thighs
and a green lacy top
showing off tits
that were hanging so far out
I could see the intimate
brown of nipple

chubby Cleopatras

ordering doner kebabs
and cheesy garlic bread

over the phone.

The Aquarium

How can you be that size?

Three piano key heads in the queue for the aquarium.

My children
two, five and seven
and mum –

my family
in the space between
the barriers

and the other people waiting to go in.

Leaves

Today is a day the leaves
fall from the trees

showing off to each other
with pirouettes and spins

leaving home for a new life
dead on the ground.

Fern

I wish I had the patience of a fern;
to watch millennia unfurl,
to watch species come and go,
to just respond to my surroundings
in the nooks and sediment of time –
to just stay true to myself
in the half-light of forever.

Hibiscus

I have got three children.
I am walking past school.
There is a Hibiscus in a front garden
flowering,
and I am trying to cry.

Breadsticks

Pincushioned by demands
from the other room

instructions called through as I cook
their dinner

I am a soldier
felled
by arrows
from an enemy

he loves.

On my knees
gasping my last words

"Hold on, OK" I say

"Yes you can have
a breadstick."

Alive

Sometimes I hang out the washing
even though I'm pretty sure it's about to rain

Sometimes I take handfuls of the potatoes I've just peeled
over to the saucepan rather than bringing
the pan over to the sink

Sometimes I turn left even though the route-planner
is telling me to keep going straight

Sometimes I wait a few seconds before replying
just to let something sink in

Sometimes I wish for something that's very unlikely
to happen, or plant a plant in winter even though
I know it will probably die

Sometimes I don't say exactly what I mean
because it's nice to be alive, sometimes.

Chinos

It's funny how misshapen chinos come about.
All of a sudden you're wearing some,
above a cheap pair of trainers.

Comma

Just look at that comma!
How dare you.
You take my breath away.

Doubt

My wildfires are really raging,
sweeping through my intestines
and up the funnel of my throat
leaving my words charred;

leaving skeletons of burnt-out
wood. Doors on hinges.
Smoking stumps as firemen pick through the remnants
of my life.

What happened here?
Was it a fuse inside me
that malfunctioned? Or the grinning arsonist
I live with?

News reports will show the teddy bears of my youth
and the springs of a mattress
consumed by heat.
I will have to rebuild again.

Without charity.
Without help.

Family Life

There's a lot of talk about
men and women,
and women and men

and sometimes it gets confusing –

all I know is

you are the blanket,
but I am the tentpole.

Greatness

I thought my moment of greatness might come when my
poems are published, or I finish my book

or if I do get a big job, after all, and not only boost
audience figures to new levels
but do so with a humility
and wisdom
that surprises all my colleagues

or, perhaps, given my age, it might be a late flourish at football
and scoring twenty goals again this season
matching the best of my thirties –

but, who knew, it would actually turn out to be replying to
my youngest son during
another episode of Blaze and the Monster Machines

and then not only deciding to go upstairs and help with bedtime
without being asked
but reading their story with everything I've got left

and then not even hurrying as I do their singing
and say goodnight.

Half term

Like mushrooms

children appear suddenly
overnight

hopping, skipping
holding hands in the street

pulling
being pulled
tugging
being tugged

bothering
spinning
hungry

a sudden doubling

enchanted,
enchanting.

Doggy style

I want to see
and feel
the exact moment
my proboscis
becomes you
from behind.

The simple back
and forth –

the slow
rhythm
and friction
of us.

Handrail

You don't understand –
all the irritation, exasperation and abuse I hurl at you
silently
as we're out and about with the children
is just a handrail to stop me
falling. Falling off the side
of this path we're on together; this path that
keeps opening up with expanses of joy
and little crunchy pebbles of delight
that are so unexpected
and overwhelming
I need to just hold on as
tight as I can.

Benches

The most middle class thing in the whole wide world is
those benches –

on Hampstead Heath
in memory of so and so

                        who lived between these dates
                        and so enjoyed this view

but is now dead.

Don't get me wrong –

I have nothing against the middle class
or benches
or Hampstead Heath

or, indeed, death.

But why does so and so's name need to be
engraved where we all have to see it

                        every time we sit down?

Or even just go for a walk.

Happiness

it is there
beneath all the torment and the envy and the pain –

a layer of colour,
just showing through

Househusband

Who am I?

I looked after Bubba today when you told me she had
a slight temperature
and needed to stay home

and Amory when he got a temperature too

but nursery called you
and then you called me
although I was driving to Tesco so I called you back
when we'd parked
and I stroked Amory's hair
and took off his shoes
and put on Cbeebies
and then Blaze
but I messaged you to ask if he needed Calpol
and called you when he cried with a tummy ache
and felt panicky and close to tears
but it was you he kept asking for
and when you came home early
everything suddenly seemed
OK.

And I am looking forward to lunch on Sunday?
Or dreading it?

I've seen it on the calendar
lunch at The Woolpack with Tamasin & Guy
but are they your friends?

Or ours?
Or mine?

I like them –
don't get me wrong
and their kids
but you introduced me to him
after talking to her at Creepy Crawlies
and now I have his number
and a twice yearly history of drinks
but is he your friend?

Or ours?
Or mine?

And he's working
and doing well
and his app is starting to make real money
but I only hunt battery-operated toys that I can't turn off
these days
and gather peas into the dustpan and brush
with the short strokes I've perfected
however I'm thinking
of becoming a teacher
at forty-eight
after quitting my job
that night
back in March
when I realised I couldn't cope.

So here I am.

I take out the rubbish
and reseal the bathroom (quite a good job last time)
and tidy the playroom most nights
but I'm pretty good-looking
in fact I'm "fucking good-looking" (you said so yourself)
but I'm not Don Draper
or even Wayne Rooney
I write poems (but haven't been published)
and haven't quite finished a book yet
(although I've been at it for twenty years)
I'm not Saddam Hussein, or Putin, so that's good
and I'm younger than Mick Jagger so further than he is
from death
and I love you all more
than I will ever
be able
to say

but I have no idea who I am

and please

don't just
tell me

I am

me.

Like

I can't remember what you were like because
you're so like you are now

I can't remember how you used to play on that
fire engine in the soft play
because you are playing on it right now

I can't remember what it felt like when we were sitting
on that bench, over there, and I tried to give you
lunch because we are sitting here now

and it has gone.

Controlled Conditions

I am experimenting with the idea of being happy –

just taking pipette-fulls of how
I'm feeling

       and squeezing them out
          very carefully,

and under extremely controlled conditions
                     into the present

      and then standing back

to see what happens.

Quiet

I came across some quiet
in the far corner
of a field
on my walk just now –

and it was wonderful.

Old Man's Chin

My chin looks old in the rear view mirror.
A bristly old man's chin

bathed in a slice of morning sun.

     A collar
       pinching

            on loosening skin

and with my left eye I can see the road lines
disappearing

       to where I once was.

Shoes

Everyone has their own feelings about their shoes.
The choice they made, in a shop
or online –
the doubts and the glory.
That ongoing dialogue.
Trainers, flats (what even are they?) heels, brogues,
boots. Are they easy to put on?
Do they make you feel tall?
Clever? Sexy? Alert?
Do you wear them with tights? With socks? With tight
trousers? Or your going out dress?
We can all see your shoes.
But only you know their story.

Pizza Express

A building where I once had sex
is being knocked down.

I saw it,
just now

as I was driving past.

       I say sex –

I'm not quite sure we technically had sex

maybe just,
for a few seconds

because I was young

and we'd both got really drunk at
              Pizza Express.

New York

Two people know me in New York.
Actually three,
Possibly even four...

Not as bad as I thought.

Me

I am a sieve.

A whale filtering rushing
plankton –

a tide of experiences

that threaten to
overwhelm
me.

The Here and Now

I can't be fucked with the past; it's too long ago
or, indeed, the future

because it never comes.

So what does that leave me?
That's right.

The here and fucking now.

Brainwave

Noticing things wrong.
Things that need changing.

Hair blocking the plug.

Certainty.

Who's fault?
Who will sort it?
When?

But why not happy things?
Because what will you think about

then?

Anxiety

What happens if you don't cut back your lavender
in autumn?

What happens if you don't chop an onion
roughly
as the recipe requires?

What happens if you use
kitchen cleaner

in the bathroom?

What happens if you leave the tap running a bit too long
while you're brushing your teeth?

Not a great deal.

Sex

all this stuff about sex

this head over heels desire
this on your knees lust

all this need

the main thing

deep down inside
is the fact that

the person you're having
sex with

is someone else

My Feelings

I labour at the chalkface of my
feelings day and night; toiling

trying to work out what
I think about this or that;

trying to work out if I
should've been more understanding

and let go, or whether, actually
I might have a point;

trying to work out what I
should do with my life;

whether I should take a risk
or just accept things for what they are.

But that's the problem.

What are they?
How do I actually feel?

Crossroads

I am at a crossroads –
every way I turn I feel happy
and I don't know what to do.

Poetry

It is not the briar
and bramble

it is the meaning –

the person who might walk through.

Singularity

the sound of my chair on the floor as I move forwards
then,
the feel of the fork in my hand
a forkful of jacket potato
then chewing, and the taste

the sound of my knife scraping the plate as I cut the chicken
then,
the movement of sitting back in my chair
allowing myself time to absorb it all

then starting again

Pram Seat

The pram we brought had a detachable plastic seat at the back.

A low throne where the children could survey
the High Street or the route to the park.

They would argue over it.

Whose go is it?
Who's been sitting on it the longest?

And they often drew comments from passers-by –

"I wish I had one of those when I was a child!"
"Aren't you the lucky one!"

Or, perhaps, just a smile.

We knew it was pretty cool but yesterday, after a couple
of brief discussions, I took it to the dump.

The bits of the pram were all apart
and I took the cradle out first

and then carried it right round to Household Goods
and then took the frame to Bay 6, as directed.

I can't remember if I took the seat by itself
or with something else

(ah, yes, it was the nappy bin)

but when I took them both over to Household Goods
and held each in each hand

I stopped –

and I still haven't cried.

Clarinet

My dad used to play the clarinet

a cautious sound
up on the top floor

or in their bedroom
downstairs
after they'd downsized.

Little snippets,
over and over again

an accent changed
a jazzy note added.

I could hear the pads of his fingers

and those reeds
he used to make himself

I could see his clarinet, too
if I went in

on that wooden stand
in the corner –

but I never actually saw him play.

Swimming

I went swimming in the Family Pool today.
With my family.

Life

So many significancies. Turned out

The Present

The present is a bar of soap.
Oops, there it goes again!

Double Bed

I think I want to sleep in a double bed with you
even though it's hard
not two singles
with separate chimney stack legs,
not spaced neatly apart and side by side
so I have to turn my head to talk to you –
but a single double mattress
an oil slick of us
that confuses and comforts me
from my own shore.

Colgate

Aliens will ask about Colgate.

How did they achieve such market dominance
and yet remain so under the radar?

And how did it all start?

It really is

something special.